UNDERSTANDING REMOVAL PROCEEDINGS IN THE IMMIGRATION COURT

Robert G. Berke

UNDERSTANDING REMOVAL PROCEEDINGS IN THE IMMIGRATION COURT

ISBN: 978-0-9849507-6-8
Library of Congress: Pending

Cover art and book design are the property of:
MultiModoMedia Press
MultiModoMedia Press is an imprint of MultiModoMedia, Inc., a California Corporation with offices located at:
21911 Sherman Way, Canoga Park, CA 91303
http://www.multimodomedia.com

Printed in the U.S.A.

DEDICATION

The United States is, was, and always will be a nation of immigrants, the brave people from across the globe who left their homes, their families, and all that they were familiar with to help us build the great nation we are today. It is to these heroes that I dedicate this book.

~ Robert G. Berke

CONTENTS

PREFACE

A removal proceeding is the legal process by which aliens can be expelled from the United States.

Thousands of aliens are placed in removal proceedings every year forcing their departure from the United States. Those placed in removal proceedings include aliens who entered the United States unlawfully, aliens who have violated their accorded status in the United States, lawful permanent residents who have committed a crime or made a material misrepresentation in an application, and asylum seekers.

According to statistics for the 2016 fiscal year:

- ***328,112 aliens were placed in Removal proceedings;***
- ***273,390 cases were completed; and***
- ***223,498 removal orders were issued.***

Source: https://www.justice.gov/eoir/page/file/fysb16/download

---

Based on these numbers only a mere 20% of aliens placed in removal proceedings are granted relief. While some aliens removed by the Immigration Court are ultimately granted relief through appellate or collateral processes, the vast majority are not. The Bureau of Immigration and Customs Enforcement (ICE), the agency responsible for enforcing removal orders, has been proactive and effective in removing aliens who are under final orders of removal. Statistically speaking, aliens whom the U.S. government seeks to deport are likely to be deported.

Aliens represented by counsel fare much better than aliens who choose to represent themselves.

> ***"Among detained immigrants, those with representation were twice as likely as unrepresented immigrants to obtain immigration relief if they sought it (49 percent with counsel versus 23 percent without)."***
>
> ***"Represented immigrants who were never detained were nearly five times more likely than their unrepresented counterparts to obtain relief if they sought it (63 percent with counsel versus 13 percent without)."***
>
> ***Source: https://www.americanimmigrationcouncil.org/research/access-counsel-immigration-court***

This book is intended to serve as an overview as to what removal proceedings are and how they are conducted as well as to provide information about the most common forms of relief. **This guide is not intended to constitute legal advice and should not be relied on as legal advice. It is neither comprehensive nor exhaustive.** Immigration law is highly complex and constantly changing and thus, any sources cited herein should be checked for currentness.

It is the author's belief that an alien in removal proceedings can better assist his attorney in defending a case before the Immigration Court if he or she better understands the process.

1 OVERVIEW OF THE IMMIGRATION COURT

The Immigration Court is an administrative court under the jurisdiction of the United States Department of Justice. It is part of a larger adjudicatory apparatus known as the Executive Office of Immigration Review (EOIR). The Executive Office of Immigration Review defines its mission as follows:

> ***"The primary mission of the Executive Office for Immigration Review (EOIR) is to adjudicate immigration cases by fairly, expeditiously, and uniformly interpreting and administering the Nation's immigration laws. Under delegated authority from the Attorney General, EOIR conducts immigration court proceedings, appellate reviews, and administrative hearings."***

Source: https://www.justice.gov/eoir

The Executive Office of Immigration Review has several agencies within it. The two agencies involved in removal proceedings are: the Immigration Court and the Board of Immigration Appeals.

The Immigration Court is a "trial court." It is the Court that hears evidence and argument and makes initial rulings on removal cases. The Board of Immigration Appeals is an "appellate court." It reviews the decisions of the Immigration Court for legal, factual, or procedural errors on the request of either the alien or the government.

If no appeal is filed at the Board of Immigration Appeals, the Immigration Court's order becomes final; however, any decision of the Immigration Court can be reviewed by the Board of Immigration Appeals (with one very narrow exception in the case of review proceedings which are discussed more at length below.) The Board of Immigration Appeals does not hear testimony, but can accept new documentary evidence under certain circumstances. The Board can either grant a case on appeal, dismiss the appeal, or remand the case to the Immigration Court for further proceedings. If the Board affirms the Immigration Court's decision, the decision of the Board is deemed to be a final administrative order of removal. Depending on the nature of the decision, a federal circuit court can review a final administrative order of removal.

2 SOURCES OF IMMIGRATION LAW

The Immigration and Nationality Act (Title 8 of the U.S. Code) is the book of laws passed by Congress to codify the policy of the United States with respect to immigration matters. The Act delegates most of the authority for the enforcement of immigration laws to the Attorney General and sets forth the instructions for the Attorney General to follow when enforcing and implementing immigration laws.

Notwithstanding the designation of the Attorney General as the enforcer of the immigration laws, the Department of Justice's role is actually quite limited as most of the enforcement function is now borne by the United States Department of Homeland Security through its United States Citizenship and Immigration Services (USCIS), Bureau of Immigration and Customs Enforcement (ICE), and Customs and Border Patrol (CBP).

The Department of Justice and the Attorney General still maintain authority over deciding who should be removed from the United States (with the exception of persons subject to expedited removal, see chapter 10).

The Immigration and Nationality Act actually only represents a small portion of the law relating to removal proceedings. A removal defense practitioner must also be conversant with Title 8 of the Code of Federal Regulations, precedent decisions of the Board of Immigration Appeals, the Circuit Courts, and the Supreme Court, state criminal laws and the cases that interpret those laws, countless policy memoranda, and the United States Constitution (contrary to popular belief, even undocumented aliens are afforded certain constitutional rights, including the right to a full and fair hearing.) Both the Immigration Court and the Board of Immigration Appeals publish practice manuals that explain the procedures to be followed in those courts.

Immigration law becomes inordinately complex because of the numerous sources of the law which sometimes appear to contradict each other.

> ***"The statutory scheme defining and delimiting the rights of aliens is exceedingly complex. Courts and commentators have stated that the Immigration and Nationality Act resembles 'King Minos's labyrinth in ancient Crete,' and is 'second only to the Internal Revenue Code in complexity.'"***
>
> ***Chan v. Reno, 1997 U.S. Dist. LEXIS 3016, *5 (S.D.N.Y. 1997) (citations omitted).***

---

3 REMOVABLE ALIENS

When the U.S. government believes that a person should not be in the United States, it files a Notice to Appear in the Immigration Court to get an order for that person to be removed from the United States. This initiates a legal process called a "removal proceeding." **In order to be subject to removal from the United States, a person must be an "alien" which is defined as a person who is not a citizen or national of the United States.** Citizenship laws are complex and the U.S. government occasionally does erroneously put a U.S. Citizen in removal proceedings. The Court must ensure that citizens do not get ordered removed.

Once an immigration court determines that a person is an alien it must then determine if the person is removable. Immigration law recognizes two general categories of aliens who are subject to removal proceedings: (1) "arriving aliens" and (2) aliens who are "present but deportable". How an alien may categorized is not always immediately obvious due to a concept called "parole admission." A parole admission permits and alien's body to enter the United States, but leaves his or her legal status outside of our borders still knocking on the door asking to come in. Asylum applicants are frequently permitted to enter the United States this way, but are still considered arriving aliens when applying for relief in the Immigration Court.

Arriving aliens must ultimately prove that the law permits them to enter the United States while aliens who have already entered, legally or illegally, must show that the law permits them to remain.

Aliens who are subject to removal proceedings come to the attention of the U.S. government in a variety of ways. Sometimes they are apprehended by the border patrol at or near the border; sometimes they are identified while serving criminal sentences; sometimes they are referred by USCIS (United States Immigration and Citizenship Service) upon the denial of an application for benefits.

The Attorney General and the Department of Homeland Security will generally publish their "enforcement priorities" and, in some administrations, will not prosecute cases that do not fit within their priorities. The current administration has announced that it will prosecute the cases of any alien it deems to be removable regardless of their priority pronouncements. This means that under the current administration students and homemakers are being treated identically to hardened criminals. It remains to be seen how this will affect the already overwhelming caseloads of the Immigration Courts. There are presently nearly 600,000 cases pending in the Immigration Court across the United States and under 400 judges to hear them all.

4 COMMENCEMENT OF PROCEEDINGS

Removal Proceedings are commenced by the filing of a Notice to Appear (NTA) in the Immigration Court. After the filing of a Notice to Appear, the Immigration Court has jurisdiction to determine if a person can be ordered removed from the United States. As stated above, the Immigration Court has no jurisdiction over U.S. Citizens. The Immigration Court is a part of the Executive Office of Immigration Review. Immigration Proceedings before the Immigration Court are adversarial in nature. The opposing parties are the Department of Homeland Security (also called "DHS" or the "Department") and the person the DHS is trying to remove (the "Respondent"). The DHS is the successor to the former INS (Immigration and Naturalization Service) and references to the INS should now be replaced by the designation DHS.

Immigration Court proceedings consist of at least three phases, each of which are discussed in detail in the following chapters. These phases are: the pleading phase, the removability phase, and the relief phase. In rare instances a case can be resolved after two or three Court dates, but it is not unusual for Immigration Court proceedings to go on for years and require multiple hearings.

In the case of detained aliens, a bond hearing will also be held at or prior to the pleading phase. Bond eligibility is discussed below in the chapter on mandatory detention.

At the conclusion of the proceedings before the Immigration Court, the Respondent or the DHS may accept the decision of the Immigration Judge or appeal the decision to the Board of Immigration Appeals (the BIA). The Board of Immigration Appeals does not conduct evidentiary hearings and merely resolves legal issues.

The Respondent or the DHS in certain instances may seek review of adverse decisions in the Federal Courts.

There are three common designations given to hearings in the Immigration Court: the master hearing, individual hearing, and merits hearing.

Master hearings are short hearings set on a Court's "master calendar" and are usually scheduled for procedural matters such as pleading to an NTA or filing an application for relief. When you appear for a master hearing, you will be on the Court's calendar with several other people, sometimes dozens of other people, and the Court will only be able to dedicate a few minutes to each case.

Individual hearings are set on a Court's "individual calendar" which is reserved longer matters, such as hearings on removability and trials on applications for relief. Though the terms are used somewhat interchangeably, the merits hearing generally refers to the trial on the ultimate form of relief sought and is set on an individual calendar.

5 THE PLEADING AND REMOVABILITY PHASES

The Notice to Appear (NTA) in the Immigration Court, which commences the proceedings contains several key elements.

First, the notice will identify that the alien is either, (1) seeking admission to the United States, (2) admitted to the United States but deportable, or (3) an alien present in the United States without having been admitted or paroled.

Second, the notice will set forth the factual allegations the government believes give it a basis to remove the alien from the United States.

Third, the notice will set forth with specificity what portion of the INA it believes gives it legal power to remove the alien from the United States.

Fourth, the notice will specify a date, time, and place for the alien to present him or herself to the Immigration Court.

The Notice to Appear also contains some very important warnings. The most critical of these warnings is the address change notification warning. Once served with the notice, the alien is required to advise the Immigration Court within five days of moving or changing address. Court dates frequently get changed and notices of such changes are sent by mail. If an alien has moved and failed to notify the Court and does not get notice of a change of court date, he or she can be ordered removed in absentia and there may be little to nothing an attorney can do to get that order reversed.

> *Failure to appear: You are required to provide the DHS, in writing, with your full mailing address and telephone number. You must notify the Immigration Court immediately by using Form EOIR-33 whenever you change your address or telephone number during the course of this proceeding. You will be provided with a copy of this form. Notices of hearing will be mailed to this address. If you do not submit Form EOIR-33 and do not otherwise provide an address at which you may be reached during proceedings, then the Government shall not be required to provide you with written notice of your hearing. If you fail to attend the hearing at the time and place designated on this notice, or any date and time later directed by the Immigratio.n Court, a removal order may be made by the immigration judge in your absence and you may be arrested and detained by the DHS.*
>
> *Excerpt from a Notice to Appear*

Finally, the Notice to Appear will contain a proof of service upon the alien showing the manner in which the notice was served.

At the initial master hearing before the Immigration Court, the judge will ask several questions regarding the Notice to Appear. The judge will ask if the alien concedes that he or she is the alien named in the Notice, whether the alien concedes that the NTA was properly served, whether the alien admits or denies the factual allegations in the NTA, and whether the alien concedes the ground or grounds of removability specified in the NTA. If the alien is represented by an attorney, the Court will ask the alien if he or she wants that attorney to speak for him or her.

It is important to recognize that the NTA is not always accurate.

Often it has been prepared by a non-attorney who is not fully aware of the specific facts of an alien's case. It is a grave mistake to assume that it is accurate and it must be reviewed carefully by an attorney before pleadings are taken. It is the government's burden to prove the factual allegations and the charged ground of removability. However, once service is acknowledged and removability is conceded, the government is relieved of its burden of proof. Even the proof of service portion contains information that may affect legal rights (i.e. "the stop-time rule").

The pleadings must be very carefully considered because an error in pleading can be fatal to a case. Not every judge will permit an alien to change his or her pleading at a later date, *especially* when the charge of removability is predicated on a criminal conviction. If there is even a hint that there is some error in the NTA, or any question about the alien's removability, it is generally better to let the judge make a finding of removability than to concede removability. This preserves the issue of removability on appeal and allows the alien to take advantage of subsequent changes in the law which arise frequently in the criminal immigration context.

If there is an issue about an alien's removability, the alien should move for a termination of his proceedings. Removal proceedings can be terminated if the government cannot prove that the alien is removable from the United States. It is not enough for the government to simply allege that an alien is removable from the United States for one reason or another. It must prove the allegation to a "clear and convincing evidence" standard. The one exception to this rule is that an alien contesting a charge of having entered the United States illegally bears the burden of proving the time, place, and manner of entry. Frequently a separate hearing on an individual calendar will be set for the presentation of such proof.

When the government believes the alien is removable on the basis of a criminal conviction, it is insufficient for the government to simply prove that a crime was committed. The government bears the burden of proving that the crime meets the definition of an offense that renders the alien removable. This is no simple task as the government must make this proof based on a closed universe of documents called the "record of conviction." The analysis for whether an offense qualifies as a removable offense is one of the most complex areas of American law.

If an alien is going to seek termination of proceedings, it is important to raise that issue at the pleading phase of the removal proceeding. It is often necessary to deny any allegations relating to the crime and also the criminal ground of removability. If removability is denied, the Judge will normally set a separate hearing just on the issue of removability. If the allegations relating to the crime are admitted or the ground of removability is conceded, the alien could waive his right to contest removability even on appeal.

If the Court determines that an alien is removable the next step is for the Court to consider available relief.

6 THE RELIEF PHASE

This section discusses the MOST COMMON forms of relief sought in the Immigration Court which are (1) LPR Cancellation of Removal; (2) Non-LPR Cancellation of Removal; (3) Adjustment and Re-Adjustment of Status; (4) Asylum, Withholding, and Deferral of Removal; (5) Former 212(c) Relief; and (6) Voluntary Departure.

1. <u>LPR Cancellation of Removal</u>

LPR Cancellation of Removal is the first form of relief from removal that we look to when we represent a legal permanent resident that has been charged as removable for having committed a criminal offense, though it can be used to cancel non-criminal grounds of removability as well.

This form of relief is governed by INA §240A(a) which states:

> *The Attorney General may cancel removal in the case of an alien who is inadmissible or deportable from the United States if the alien-*

(1) has been an alien lawfully admitted for permanent residence for not less than 5 years,

(2) has resided in the United States continuously for 7 years after having been admitted in any status, and

(3) has not been convicted of any aggravated felony.

Issues involving the "stop-time rule" which calculates the date on which a lawful admission or continuous residence is deemed to end and whether an offense is an aggravated felony arise frequently when this relief is sought. If a judge finds that the alien meets the statutory eligibility requirement, the decision whether to grant the relief is purely discretionary. It is helpful to envision a scale: on one side of the scale are all of the reasons that the government is seeking removal and on the other side of the scale are all of the good reasons that the alien should be permitted to stay. If the good reasons to let the alien stay outweigh the reasons to remove him, he will likely win his case. HOWEVER, because it is discretionary, a judge may not grant the relief if he or she thinks the alien is being dishonest or is likely to commit future crimes. For this reason, candor and rehabilitation are important considerations.

2. Non-LPR Cancellation of Removal

The statute governing Cancellation of Removal for aliens who are not legal permanent residents is far more complex and restrictive. This form of relief is governed by INA §240A(b) which states:

---

(1) IN GENERAL.-The Attorney General may cancel removal of, and adjust to the status of an alien lawfully admitted for permanent residence, an alien who is inadmissible or deportable from the United States if the alien-

(A) has been physically present in the United

> States for a continuous period of not less than 10 years immediately preceding the date of such application;
>
> (B) has been a person of good moral character during such period;
>
> (C) has not been convicted of an offense under section 212(a)(2), 237(a)(2) , or 237(a)(3) , subject to paragraph (5); and
>
> (D) establishes that removal would result in exceptional and extremely unusual hardship to the alien's spouse, parent, or child, who is a citizen of the United States or an alien lawfully admitted for permanent residence.

Generally, the most difficult aspect of this form of relief is the "exceptional and extremely unusual hardship" standard. This standard has been difficult for the Courts to define, but certain guidelines have been established through appellate proceedings (see, ie, Matter of Monreal, 23 I&N Dec. 56 (BIA 2001); Matter of Andazola-Rivas, 23 I&N Dec. 319 (BIA 2002); Matter of Recinas, 23 I&N Dec. 467 (BIA 2002)).

As a general proposition, an alien seeking this form of relief should be able to demonstrate hardships to the pertinent relative or relatives that go beyond the normal hardships an alien facing deportation would face. The normal hardships include separation of the family, economic setbacks, educational interruptions, and sadness. Exceptional hardships must be greater than these. The law requires an Immigration Judge to consider all the hardships an alien would face "in the aggregate." Accordingly, all the hardships to all the qualifying relatives should be raised and considered.

Aliens with criminal convictions frequently find themselves ineligible for this form of relief under either prong (B) or prong (C). Courts of Appeal have held that aliens who are either deportable OR inadmissible based on criminal activity are ineligible for this form of relief. Gonzalez-Gonzalez v. Ashcroft, 390 F.3d 649 (9th Cir. 2004). Furthermore, many crimes make it difficult or impossible to prove "good moral character." See INA 101(f).

Another pitfall hidden within the statute is the "stop-time rule" which states that the period of continuous physical presence referred to in subsection (A) above is deemed to end, "when the alien has committed an offense referred to in section 212(a)(2) that renders the alien inadmissible to the United States under section 212(a)(2) or removable from the United States under section 237(a)(2) or 237(a)(4), whichever is earliest." INA §240A(d). The proper service of a Notice to Appear in the Immigration Court also stops the accrual of time toward the period of continuous physical presence. For this reason, the validity of both the Notice to Appear and the manner of service of the Notice to Appear should be investigated prior to any acknowledgement of proper service. For these reasons, even aliens who have resided in the United States for decades may not qualify for this form of relief based on their failure to accrue the necessary time.

There are also some special forms of cancellation of removal for certain aliens including persons from El Salvador and Guatemala who applied for certain benefits in or before 1989 and for persons who have been victims of domestic violence in the United States.

The Immigration Court can only grant 40,000 of these applications annually. If the Immigration Judge is inclined to grant the case, but the 40,000 annual cap has already been reached, the judge cannot enter a decision and will normally continue the matter into the following fiscal year.

3. **Adjustment and Re-Adjustment of Status**

Adjustment of Status (INA §245) is the process by which an alien already present in the United States can become a legal permanent resident of the United States. In order to qualify, the alien must have either an approved family petition, an approved self-petition, or an approved labor certification and the immigrant visa must be available. Furthermore, the alien must either have the benefit of INA §245(i)[which is a complex topic on its own] or in the case of immediate relatives, a lawful admission. Even people who are already legal permanent residents of the United States are eligible to apply for adjustment again as there are certain waivers available in the adjustment context that are not otherwise available. In order to re-adjust, an alien must obtain a new immigrant (family, labor, self) petition.

Aliens with crimes who are otherwise eligible to adjust their status in the United States may require a special waiver. The waiver is not available to aliens who have been convicted of most drug crimes other than simple possession of less than 30 grams of marijuana. Non-drug related crimes involving moral turpitude can be waived. Non-drug crimes that do not involve moral turpitude do not have to be waived as they do not in general trigger a ground of inadmissibility. When an alien is convicted of only one crime involving moral turpitude for which the maximum sentence is under a year and the actual sentence is under 180 days, no waiver is needed. This is called the petty offense exception.

The waiver itself is codified at INA §212(h) and is requested by the filing of a form I-601. INA §212(h) has two distinct parts. The first part relates to offenses that are over fifteen years old which can be waived with no threshold hardship requirement. The second part relates to newer convictions and requires a showing of extreme hardship to qualifying a relative. A similar waiver, codified at INA §212(i) can be applied in cases involving fraud or misrepresentation when there has been no criminal conviction.

Though the term "aggravated felony" is generally irrelevant in the adjustment context because it is not a ground of inadmissibility, an aggravated felony will render certain aliens ineligible for the 212(h) waiver. The Courts have limited that ineligibility to aliens who entered the United States as legal permanent residents. Also, aliens who have been convicted of murder or crimes involving torture are ineligible for the waiver unless they initially entered the United States before April 1990.

Practitioners should also be aware of 8 CFR §212.7(d) which raises the burden in 212(h) cases when the alien has been convicted of "violent or dangerous crimes".

The Attorney General, in general, will not favorably

> *exercise discretion under section 212(h)(2) of the Act (8 U.S.C. 1182(h)(2)) to consent to an application or reapplication for a visa, or admission to the United States, or adjustment of status, with respect to immigrant aliens who are inadmissible under section 212(a)(2) of the Act in cases involving violent or dangerous crimes, except in extraordinary circumstances, such as those involving national security or foreign policy considerations, or cases in which an alien clearly demonstrates that the denial of the application for adjustment of status or an immigrant visa or admission as an immigrant would result in exceptional and extremely unusual hardship. Moreover, depending on the gravity of the alien's underlying criminal offense, a showing of extraordinary circumstances might still be insufficient to warrant a favorable exercise of discretion under section 212(h)(2) of the Act.*
>
> *8 CFR 212.7(d)*

---

4. Asylum, Withholding, and Deferral of Removal

These three forms of relief from removal are significantly similar in that they all hinge on conditions in the alien's country of citizenship. Asylum can be asserted both affirmatively and defensively, while withholding and deferral under the Convention Against Torture (CAT) are defensive applications. These applications are sometimes referred to as political based relief or I-589 relief (referring to the form on which all three forms of relief are requested).

Asylum and withholding of removal differ only in regards to the burden of proof required and the actual relief that is granted. Both of these forms of relief require proof that the alien has been or will be persecuted on account of being a member of a protected class (race, religion, ethnicity, national origin, political opinion, or "membership in a particular social group").

Deferral under the Convention Against Torture differs in that it requires proof that the alien will be tortured in his country of citizenship by the government or with government acquiescence but does not require that the torture would be meted out for any particular reason. The alien does not need to be a member of a protected class in order to qualify for this relief.

Asylum can be barred to an alien in Removal proceedings due to criminal convictions or because the application was not filed within one year of the alien's arrival in the United States. Withholding can be barred to an alien who has been convicted of a "particularly serious crime". There are no crimes that bar an alien from seeking relief under the Convention Against Torture.

A grant of asylum creates a path to residency and citizenship. A grant of withholding or deferral under the Convention Against Torture does not. In fact, those two forms of relief do not even prevent the entry of an order of removal, they simply prevent the execution of the order of removal.

5. Former 212(c)

This section of the INA was repealed in 1996, but the Courts have held that in certain circumstances the repeal of this section was "impermissibly retroactive." Aliens who were either in proceedings before April 1997 or who had committed crimes prior to April 1997 should seek counsel to determine whether they may possibly qualify for this relief as it was available to waive offenses which cannot be waived with LPR-Cancellation of Removal. If an alien qualifies for this ground of relief, it is purely discretionary with the Immigration Judge as to whether it will be granted.

6. Voluntary Departure

An alien in removal proceedings can also ask for permission to leave the United States voluntarily either at the beginning of Court proceedings if he does not have relief available or at the end of his Court proceedings if relief has been denied. Aliens who may wish to immigrate in the future can benefit by agreeing to depart voluntarily as the entry of a removal order can interfere with future processes. The Immigration Judge will normally set a bond for voluntary departure to ensure that the alien abides by the agreement. The bond must be paid within five days. A judge can grant up to four months to leave the country if voluntary departure is requested at the beginning of proceedings and up to two months if it is requested at the end of proceedings.

Failing to abide by a voluntary departure order renders an alien ineligible to adjust status and for some other forms of relief. In some jurisdictions, these consequences don't attach if the bond is not posted; however, an alien should never request voluntary departure unless he definitely intends to abide by the order.

Appealing the denial of a form of relief will normally stay the voluntary departure while the appeal is pending providing that the bond has been posted.

7. Administrative, Obsolete, and Rarer Forms of Relief

For many years prior to the current administration in Washington, Immigration Judges had expansive administrative powers which helped them to control their dockets and to prioritize cases. One of these powers was the power to "administratively close" proceedings when it was in the best interest of justice to do so. Common reasons for courts to administratively close matters were: because there is a pending petition before another agency or some other agency has granted (or could grant) a temporary reprieve from deportation, such as Temporary Protected Status or Deferred Action for Childhood Arrivals. Even though the Court has been divested of this power, there are still many cases that remain "administratively closed." Administratively closed cases can be reopened at any time upon the request of the alien, the government, or the Court.

When an alien is eligible to adjust his status or has a provisional stateside waiver available it used to be common for the Judge to terminate the Court case so that the USCIS can adjudicate the adjustment application. The Court still has the power to do so, but is presently restricted in doing so unless the government agrees. This does create problems in provisional stateside waiver cases.

INA §237(a)(1)(H) can be used to waive errors and misrepresentations made at the time of admission and is frequently used when the wrong immigrant visa category was selected.

Aliens who entered the United States prior to 1972 and have

never held legal status are eligible for a form of relief called Registry. Unlike amnesty, Registry remains available to use both affirmatively and defensively.

Prior to the revisions to immigration law made in 1996, there was a form of relief called suspension of deportation which was a much easier form of relief to win than Non-LPR Cancellation of Removal. Anyone who was served with papers to appear in the Immigration Court prior to October 1996 is technically not in removal proceedings but rather in deportation proceedings and may still apply for this form of relief.

Before October 1996, there were two distinct types of cases heard in the Immigration Court: one was called deportation proceedings and the other was called exclusion proceedings. After 1996, these two distinct types of proceedings were amalgamated under the singular designation of removal proceedings. Proceedings that were initiated before October 1996 were initiated by the service and filing of an Order to Show Cause (OSC), which contained almost all of the same information as a modern Notice to Appear (NTA). The distinction is important because there are certain forms of relief that no longer exist in the law, but which may still be used if the case was initiated with an OSC.

---

7 AFTER TRIAL

After hearing the evidence, unless the case was administratively closed or terminated, the Immigration Court will render a decision either granting or denying any applications for relief. The Court's decision is not a final decision. Both the alien and the government have the right to appeal any decision of the Immigration Court to the Board of Immigration Appeals. Only if the case is not appealed does the judge's decision becomes the final administrative order. This means that the Court's order cannot be enforced while the case is on appeal.

An appeal to the Board of Immigration Appeals must be received by the Board within 30 days of the judge's decision. This deadline is "jurisdictional." That means that if the Board does not receive the Notice of Appeal in time, the alien loses his right to appeal.

There are times when an appeal is inappropriate and an attorney may choose to do a motion to reopen or a motion to reconsider a decision of either the Immigration Court or the Board of Immigration Appeals. A motion to reopen seeks to introduce new evidence that could not have been produced before the end of the trial and must be filed within 90 days of the decision. A motion to reconsider is used to bring factual or legal errors in a Court's decision to the Court's attention. These motions can be brought directly to the Court if there has been no appeal filed or to the Board if an appeal has been filed. If a post-trial motion is filed in the Court, it does not stop the clock for filing an appeal. However, the denial of a post-trial motion can also be appealed to the Board.

In limited circumstances, the alien (but not the government) can ask a Circuit Court to review an adverse decision made by the Board of Immigration Appeals by filing a Petition for Review in the appropriate circuit. The filing of a Petition for Review does not automatically stop the execution of an order of removal, but a circuit court does have the power to consider a "stay of removal" upon a petitioner's request.

Neither an appeal nor a post-trial motion will stop the clock for posting a voluntary departure bond. The bond must be paid within five days if the judge granted voluntary departure.

Depending on what has been granted, there may be actions that need to be taken to secure the benefit granted by the Court. For instance, if a Court grants adjustment of status, an appointment must still be made with USCIS to have them issue the proof of status ("green card"). If asylum is granted, an application for adjustment of status must be filed with USCIS one year after the grant.

8 ALIENS WITH CRIMES

Criminal Immigration issues arise both in applications for benefits and in defense against government enforcement actions.

Applications for benefits include: requests for admission as an immigrant, requests for admission as a non-immigrant, and requests for special statuses such as temporary protected status.

Defenses against enforcement actions include: applications for relief in removal (deportation and exclusion) proceedings, expedited removal, and detention.

Fortunately, almost all crimes which have immigration consequences in all of these contexts are described in only two statutes: INA §237(a)(2) which describes offenses that render an alien deportable, and INA §212(a)(2) which describes offenses that render an alien inadmissible. The two statutes are quite different. The most striking difference is that the concept of "aggravated felony" is a ground of deportability, but not a ground of inadmissibility.

A case may involve either either admissibility or deportability. Often a case will involve both admissibility AND deportability. An example of a case that involves admissibility would involve an alien who has married a United States Citizen and would like to enter the United States to reside here permanently. An example of a case involving deportability would involve an alien who has already been admitted to the United States as a lawful permanent resident and has been residing in the United States for many years. An example of a case involving both issues of admissibility and deportability would be an alien who entered the United States lawfully, committed a crime while in the United States, and seeks to adjust his status as a form of relief from removal.

Once it is determined whether admissibility or deportability is in issue, the next step is to compare the statute of conviction to the descriptions of the criminal offenses in the INA. This is the most difficult step in the process and one which absolutely requires competent legal counsel. A very complex analysis has developed over many years of litigation for exercising this process. When comparing the statute of conviction to the crimes covered by the INA we look to see whether it is a "categorical match" which means that the conviction could not be sustained without having engaged in the exact criminal conduct described in the INA. To aid this analysis, the Courts have held that the crimes described in the INA are intended to be understood in their "generic" sense and have set forth a process for determining the generic definition of the crime. This analysis has resulted in some counterintuitive but very powerful results. For instance, a conviction for "grand theft" under California law does not categorically match the generic definition of a "theft" under the INA because California has gone beyond the generic definition of theft in its statute to punish a broader range of conduct.

If the statute of conviction is not a categorical match to the definition in the INA, it must next be determined whether the statute of conviction is "divisible" or "overbroad". A statute is divisible if it punishes separate kinds of crimes. A statute is overbroad if simply articulates different means of committing the same crime. If the statute is overbroad, it cannot be used as a ground of removability. If the statute is divisible, the Court may look to the "record of conviction" to determine which of the crimes described in the statute guilt was actually predicated on.

Again, these are tasks that require competent legal counsel.

For purposes of removability, the government bears the burden of proof and thus an inconclusive record favors the alien. For purposes of relief or affirmative benefits, the alien bears the burden of proof and thus an inconclusive record could be fatal. This differs from circuit to circuit.

There are two special categories of crimes: Aggravated Felonies and Crimes Involving Moral Turpitude. These two categories make up the bulk of criminal removal cases, but are just two of many different categories of crime that can render an alien removable. They are also two of the most misunderstood concepts in immigration law.

<u>Aggravated Felonies</u>

The term "aggravated felony" is a "term of art," which means that it does not necessarily follow a commonly understood meaning. Accordingly, there are crimes that are not felonies which qualify as aggravated felonies and similarly there are crimes which are not aggravated that qualify as aggravated felonies. The term is defined at INA §101(a)(43) and lists 21 categories of crimes in addition to attempts and conspiracies to commit the listed crimes. Aggravated Felonies bar most Respondents from most, but not all forms of discretionary relief.

The two forms of discretionary relief that still apply are:

(1) 212(c): If you were convicted of your crime before 1990 this form of relief remains available for most offenses, including aggravated felonies. If the offense was between 1990 and 1997, there is a dynamic area of case law which may provide for the availability of 212(c) relief. If the crime was committed after April 1997, there is some authority that permits for the application in VERY, VERY narrow circumstances.

and

(2) Adjustment of status: A person who has either never been a legal permanent resident of the United States or who adjusted status after entering the United States can obtain a waiver of most criminal offenses including aggravated felonies (other than 101(a)(43)(b)). See <u>In Re: Sidney</u>

Michel and Matter of J-H-J-, 26 I.&N. Dec. 563 (BIA 2015) .

Aggravated Felonies, if they are deemed "particularly serious," may bar relief in the form of Withholding of Removal. Neither Aggravated Felonies nor "particularly serious crimes" bar relief under the convention against torture.

Crimes Involving Moral Turpitude

The term "crime involving moral turpitude" is not a term of art. It means what it says. Unfortunately, the concept of "moral turpitude" is one that is inextricably intertwined with prevailing societal norms and thus cannot be perfectly defined. The definition for moral turpitude provided in the USCIS Policy Manual is, "...conduct that shocks the public conscience as being inherently base, vile, or depraved, contrary to the rules of morality and the duties owed between man and man, either one's fellow man or society in general." Case law has adopted this definition with some variation. It is safe to say that crimes that have an actual element of fraud or theft always involve moral turpitude. Generally, regulatory offenses never involve moral turpitude. The only way one can be certain that a particular crime involves moral turpitude is to roll up one's sleeves and do the research to see if any Court has already made the determination. If no Court has already made the determination, it is up to the Immigration Judge.

Collateral Attack on Conviction

Sometimes the only mechanism for solving a criminal immigration case is to return to the Court of conviction in order to vacate or alter a criminal conviction.

EXPUNGEMENTS (and other forms of rehabilitative relief) DO NOT ERADICATE THE CRIME FOR IMMIGRATION PURPOSES.[There is a narrow exception to this rule within the jurisdiction of the 9th Circuit for first time simple possession offenses from before July 14, 2011]. In fact, expunging a conviction could potentially make it more difficult to vacate later. Nonetheless, the fact that a crime has been expunged can favorably influence certain discretionary decisions.

In order to be effective for immigration purposes the

conviction needs to be vacated based on a legal, constitutional, or procedural error. Common mechanisms for doing this include:

Statutory Motions (in California, we have some very powerful statutory motions specifically designed to benefit aliens. Examples are California Penal Code sections 1016.5, 1473.3 , and 1203.43);

Common Law Motions which include the Writ of Habeas Corpus and the Writ of Error Coram Nobis.

Sometimes the conviction does not need to vacated but merely altered. This has become less of a necessity in California since the enactment of Cal. Pen. C. §18.5 which automatically modified certain misdemeanor convictions. However, it is important to know that a sentence modification IS effective for immigration purposes (Matter of Song).

Sentence and Conviction

The terms "Sentence" and "Conviction" are terms of art under the Immigration and Nationality Act. As such, do not assume that what you understand these terms to mean necessarily holds true in the Immigration context.

The terms "Sentence" and "Term of Imprisonment," significantly, include any portion of the sentence which has been suspended. This is why people with minor crimes who actually served little or no time in jail suddenly find themselves labeled as aggravated felons when placed in Removal proceedings.

The terms are discussed at section 101(a)(48)(A) and (B) of the Immigration and Nationality Act as follows:

> (A) The term "conviction" means, with respect to an alien, a formal judgment of guilt of the alien entered by a court or, if adjudication of guilt has been withheld, where-(i) a judge or jury has found the alien guilty or the alien has entered a plea of guilty or nolo contendere or has admitted sufficient facts to warrant a finding of guilt, and
> (ii) the judge has ordered some form of punishment, penalty, or restraint on the alien's

liberty to be imposed.

(B) Any reference to a term of imprisonment or a sentence with respect to an offense is deemed to include the period of incarceration or confinement ordered by a court of law regardless of any suspension of the imposition or execution of that imprisonment or sentence in whole or in part.

---

9 DETENTION AND CUSTODY

U.S. Immigration authorities have the power to arrest and detain aliens who are in the United States without permission or have violated some condition of their permission to be in the United States. The power to detain aliens derives from Immigration and Nationality Act (INA) section 236 which addresses circumstances in which an alien MAY be detained and circumstances under which an alien MUST be detained pending Immigration Court or administrative proceedings.

Most aliens who are taken into custody are eligible to be released on a bond or sometimes with only a promise to appear when requested to do so. In addition, most jurisdictions now have several "alternatives to detention" options including Supervised Release, Intensive Supervision, and electronic monitoring (ankle bracelet).

Certain aliens are not eligible to be released from custody and are deemed to be "mandatory detainees." Generally, mandatory detainees are aliens convicted of certain crimes. The following classes of alien are mandatory detainees:

(A) is inadmissible by reason of having committed any

> offense covered in section 1182(a)(2) of this title,
>
> (B) is deportable by reason of having committed any offense covered in section 1227(a)(2)(A)(ii), (A)(iii), (B), (C), or (D) of this title,
>
> (C) is deportable under section 1227(a)(2)(A)(i) of this title on the basis of an offense for which the alien has been sentence 1 to a term of imprisonment of at least 1 year, or
>
> (D) is inadmissible under section 1182(a)(3)(B) of this title or deportable under section 1227(a)(4)(B) of this title...

Aliens who have previously been deported or are currently under a final order of removal may find themselves ineligible for a bond under the statutory provisions as well.

The U.S. Courts have struggled for many years with the concept of mandatory detention which, in some instances, can amount to indefinite or even lifetime detention. Over the years numerous cases have come and gone which bear on who can be detained and for how long. This has also resulted in regional differences in how long-term detention is handled. Immigration detainees actually have far fewer rights and procedural protections than convicted criminals in criminal custody. This is because immigration detention is a "civil" detention and the detainees are not considered prisoners. Accordingly, the rights of prisoners do not necessarily adhere to immigration detainees. There has even been judicial debate over whether immigration detainees can avail themselves of the Writ of Habeas Corpus. If there is an issue over a long-term detention it is crucial to speak with an experienced immigration attorney in the region in which you are detained.

There are also jurisdictional issues relating to detention. ICE (Immigration and Customs Enforcement) has the initial opportunity to set a bond or other conditions of release after an alien is taken into custody. An Immigration Judge can then review any custody determination made by ICE. However, an Immigration Judge has no statutory authority to set a bond for an alien designated as an arriving alien.

The main considerations for Immigration Judges in making

bond determinations are the risk of flight and the alien's danger to the community. Aliens can be considered high flight risks if they have no relief available to them in the Immigration Court, no community ties, a history of immigration violations, or other factors that might cause the judge to think the alien will not show up for court or for deportation. Aliens can be considered dangerous to the community if they have a history of crimes. Even a single conviction for driving under the influence of alcohol can result in the denial of a bond on this ground.

Recent case law mandates that Immigration Judges take an alien's ability to pay a bond into consideration when setting a bond.

10 EXTRAORDINARY PROCEEDINGS

There are numerous types of proceedings which can be heard in the Immigration Court that do not follow the typical scheme for Removal Proceedings.

Immigration Courts can be called upon to conduct reinstatement proceedings. Reinstatement proceedings occur when an alien has previously been removed or deported from the United States. In such cases, the Immigration Judge need only consider whether the old order relates to the same alien and whether the old order was valid.

Sometimes, an alien previously removed or deported is encountered at the border attempting to re-enter the United States. If that alien can demonstrate that he has a reasonable fear of return to his home country, he can be placed in "asylum only" proceedings.

Aliens who have never been admitted for lawful permanent residence who are convicted of aggravated felonies in the United States, but who can demonstrate a reasonable fear of return, may be placed in "withholding only" proceedings.

The process for the above categories of aliens is called "expedited removal." Expedited removal is a process whereby a DHS officer, is authorized to enter an order of removal before the alien ever gets to see a judge. In these cases, unless the alien expresses a fear of returning to his home country, he will be deported from the United States forthwith. Absent an articulation of such fear, the only recourse the alien has is to challenge the expedited removal order in a Circuit Court. If the alien does express a fear of returning to his home country, then he is screened by an asylum officer to determine whether such fear is credible or reasonable depending on the circumstances. If the fear is found credible, the alien can be placed in asylum-only proceedings. If ineligible for asylum, but the fear is found reasonable, then the alien can be placed in withholding-only proceedings. If the fear is not found credible or reasonable, the alien can request that an immigration judge review the screen interview.

Immigration Judges also have the authority to review the findings of asylum officers who conduct reasonable fear and credible fear interviews in review proceedings. Review proceedings are unique in that the judge does not have to accept any evidence, testimony, or argument other than what appears in the asylum officer's report. These cases cannot be appealed to the Board of Immigration Appeals, but can be reviewed in a Circuit Court upon the filing of a Petition for Review.

11 HIRING AN IMMIGRATION LAWYER

A Google (TM) search for "immigration lawyer los angeles" turns up over 1,000,000 results. Not every immigration lawyer is right for every client. It is important to do your research before hiring an immigration lawyer to represent you in removal proceedings.

An excellent place to start a search for a qualified immigration lawyer is with the American Immigration Lawyers Association (AILA). Attorneys who are members of AILA are generally dedicated to the practice of immigration law, have met certain eligibility requirements, and are kept current on issues relating to the practice of immigration law. AILA has a website where you can search for an immigration lawyer according to their specific practice areas, locality, and languages spoken.

Experience is a second important criteria to look for when seeking an immigration lawyer. Experience cannot always just be measured in years. There is a difference between having 25 years of experience and having one year of experience 25 times. Attorneys who have a proven track record in multiple case types and across different courts will generally be capable of more nuanced representation than those that limit themselves to one particular case type or court.

It is normally preferable to have an attorney who is local to both you and to the court that is hearing the matter, though this is not always possible. Especially in cases in which there are criminal issues, it is preferable that the attorney be admitted to practice in the state where those crimes occurred as issues of state criminal law can be inextricably intertwined with issues of immigration law.

Personality should play a huge role in the selection of an immigration attorney. Immigration cases can take years to complete, and open and clear communication between the attorney and the client is perhaps the most important factor in determining the success or failure of an immigration case.

Do not hire a law firm before meeting the attorney personally and confirming that he or she has experience in handling your specific type of case. Especially in large urban areas, many attorneys have "arrangements" with non-attorney immigration consultants, petition preparers, or "notarios". These arrangements are illegal. Meeting your attorney in court for the first time is not acceptable. Paying a non-attorney to ensure that you have an attorney in court is not acceptable and violates attorney ethical conduct rules. In much of Latin America, a "notario" is a designation that confers special legal powers on the individual holding that title. In the United States, a "notary" has only the power to affirm a signature and requires almost no legal training or specialized knowledge.

Recommendations from friends and family are valuable, but should not be dispositive. Not all cases are alike.

Most, but not all, experienced immigration lawyers will charge at least a nominal fee for a consultation. Be prepared to pay for a consultation. In immigration law, more so than in most other areas of law, the consultation is all the client needs and there will be no "case" for the attorney to open. Absent a consultation fee, the attorney may feel more inclined to do work that is unnecessary or withhold giving valuable advice or analysis. Make sure you bring ALL available paperwork to your consultation. An attorney can give you better and more accurate advice the more he knows about your case. Particularly in immigration matters, what happened in the past is critical to what can be done in the future. So gather every document you can and bring them to your consultation.

Immigration consultations vary from attorney to attorney. At Berke Law Offices, Inc., we have historically charged $100 for a standard consultation. Immigration cases can range in price from a few hundred dollars to tens of thousands of dollars depending on many, many factors. It is common for immigration lawyers to charge flat-rates for their services. When comparing flat-rates, make sure you understand what is and is not included in a flat rate. At Berke Law Offices, Inc., we charge flat rates for most matters. We also offer payment terms for our fees. Flat rates tend to be lower than attorney's hourly rates. Depending on the locale, an experienced immigration attorney may charge between $200 and $500 per hour.

COMMONLY USED ACRONYMS

AG: Attorney General

AOS: Adjustment of Status

BIA: Board of Immigration Appeals

CAT: Convention Against Torture

CBP: Customs and Border Patrol

CFR: Code of Federal Regulations

CIMT: Crime Involving Moral Turpitude

DHS: Department of Homeland Security

DOJ: Department of Justice

EOIR: Executive Office for Immigration Review

ICE: Immigration and Customs Enforcement

IJ: Immigration Judge

INA: Immigration and Nationality Act

INS: (former) Immigration and Naturalization Service

LPR: Legal Permanent Resident

MTV: Motion to Vacate

NTA: Notice to Appear

PSC: Particularly Serious Crime

PSG: Particular Social Group

OSC: Order to Show Cause

USC: U.S. Code

USC: U.S. Citizen

USCIS: U.S. Citizenship and Immigration Service

VD: Voluntary Departure

ABOUT THE AUTHOR

Robert G. Berke is an attorney who has been licensed to practice law in the State of California since 1990. In that time he has dedicated his career to representing aliens in both immigration and criminal courts. Berke Law Offices, Inc. is located in Canoga Park, California and presently consists of four licensed attorneys and six support staff.

A graduate of the State University of New York at Albany and the Southwestern University College of Law, Mr. Berke currently resides in southern California and has written extensively on criminal and immigration issues.

Made in the USA
Monee, IL
13 September 2026

62979554R00030